Illuminate Within

Illuminate Within

Nyemah

Printed in the United States of America

Publishing services by Selah Publishing Group, LLC, Tennessee.
The views expressed or implied in this work do not necessarily
reflect those of Selah Publishing Group.

ISBN: 978-1-58930-281-5
Library of Congress Control Number: 2011961804

Introduction

I lluminate Within is a collection of sayings full of practical wisdom and truth. Inspired by the many hardships Nyemah was forced to endure in his lifetime, the sayings are result of his years of searching for truth, dealing with issues of life and finding happiness and success. The motivation of each saying is to encourage others to obtain happiness and full control over their lives as the author has experienced in his. Even as God created the earth through His spoken words, Nyemah's sayings undergird a simple truth— what we speak creates our world and affects each individual destiny. We were not created to be victimized by our circumstances, but were created to take control of them. Words are powerful. We are what we speak and believe about ourselves. Your ability to overcome starts within yourself and what you believe about yourself. You are a force, God's creative miracle. Take charge!

What you ask GOD to do He will do. Your power on the earth is all imbedded in knowing GOD

What you really deserve from love
you should not have to ask for.
Father and Mother,
when you disrespect your children,
their loved ones will be the victims

If you cannot find the character of a person...look at his friends

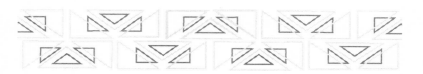

I'd rather be naked and embarrassed,
so you can see the truth,
than to wear rags of lies...
fabrics of deceit

*You cannot hide your wound
and expect it to heal*

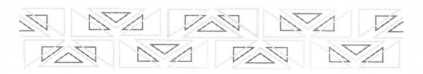

The last thing a person in hiding
will look for is light

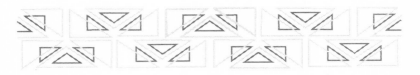

I realize survival is taking every situation the way it is...not how it should be...letting go all my inhibitions...so that happiness begins

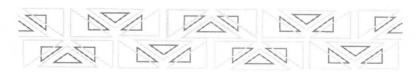

*A really bad wound will need
a stronger love portion*

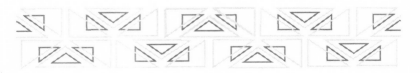

*Amongst rotten fruit
there are a few good ones...
keep digging*

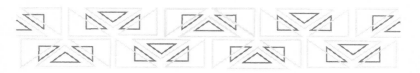

I didn't just build my house on solid ground,
but storm proofed it as well

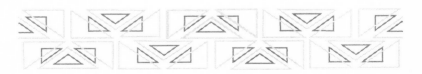

A gossip tongue is more dangerous than a wicked tongue

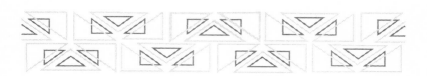

*A hippo in a swamp is not bothered when a
crocodile screams...respect one another*

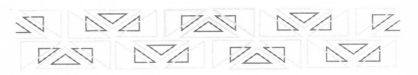

We must judge a man by the work of his heart,
not by the work of his mouth

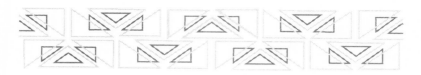

*Never remember where you fell,
only where you got up*

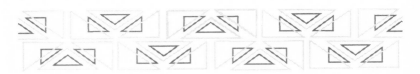

When carrying good news it is always good for you to enjoy the journey step by step

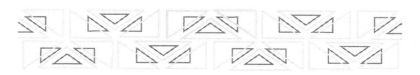

I'm amazed when my friends go and grab life by her hands...whispering in her ears...my name is somebody, but my mom calls me defeated, you can call me the same...let's seek a new beginning forgetting yesterday's limitations

*Building prisons, architect a subtle imagination
of what our reality would be*

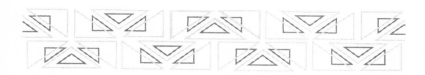

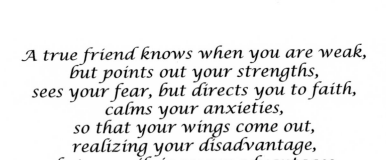

A true friend knows when you are weak,
but points out your strengths,
sees your fear, but directs you to faith,
calms your anxieties,
so that your wings come out,
realizing your disadvantage,
but magnifying your advantages

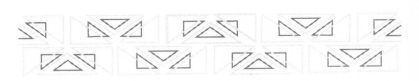

*Night and day,
hope and truth,
is what life is made of*

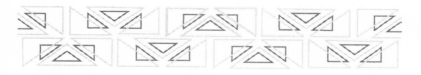

It doesn't matter what they call you...it only matters how you answer
The future belongs to those that made up their beds today

As a boy in Africa I always carried stones in my pocket, for breaking nuts, stoning mangos, and protection from stray animals

In order to catch a big stingray fish you will
need a bigger bait

In order to cross the jungle you will need to
respect the lions…and definitely you will not
need D&G fragrance

If you keep praying for rain don't be surprised if
you find your clothes wet

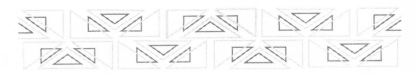

A baby chick has no right to go out dancing
with the rooster

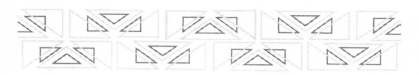

Glass has no reason to go play with rocks

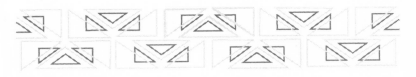

Picture a gorilla calling her baby ugly...never

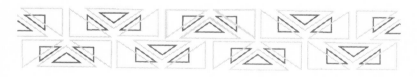

Martha Stewart has nothing,
on the floor I slept as a refugee
in Sierra Leone,
I anticipate enjoyment,
so enjoyment I have

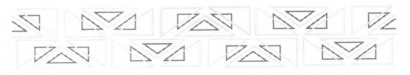

Gas and fire don't sleep in the same bed

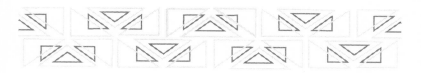

For the sake of building prisons we paint an abstract art of our own minds, where steel lives

He who dates more than two women dates himself...and is in the business section called exploitation...on lost and found page...

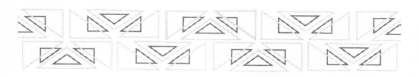

Talking to a desperate soul
is like pulling the tail of a sleeping dog

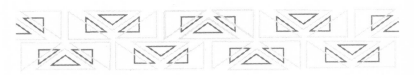

*Make sure you chew and swallow your rice
before putting another spoon in your mouth*

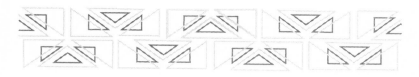

I loved the breeze
and always wanted to catch flies

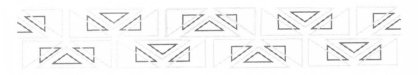

A mirror's only word is the truth

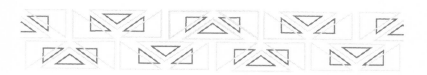

One finger cannot hold your hands together

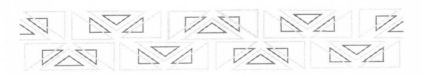

*A wonderful suit
doesn't mean a clean under garment*

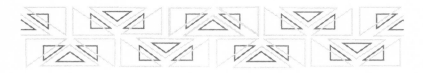

Sugar never says...damn I'm sweet

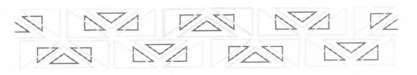

The dead know the value of words

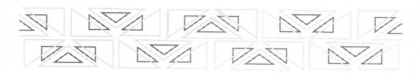

The cow that has too many owners will eventually lose its value

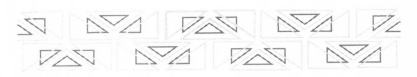

If I'm making it my business to tell you about your steps toward your destiny, it's only because I care…maybe I'm doing it wrong, but fight is the fruit I look for

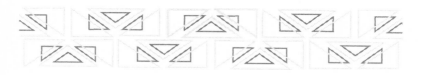

*A rich man has one thing in common with a
poor man, they both know hunger*

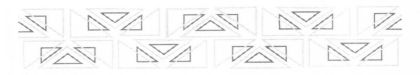

My pockets might be empty but my heart is full of seeds

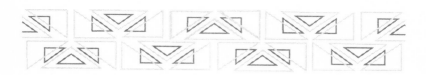

Faith's dreams are happiness,
Fool's dreams are paying the bills...

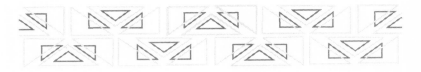

*Grandma says leopards don't change their
spots even when it rains*

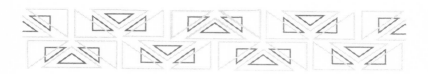

In Liberia it is said "when a dog barks it's not about the fight, but fright"

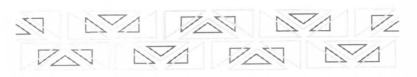

When an angry man threatens to put poison in
your food you may still eat...
but when a woman does...don't eat

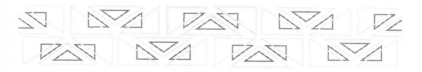

*If a person is lending you a shirt
don't say his shirt smells*

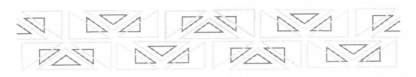

No matter how long the night seems
day will break and the rooster will tell me
"don't put all your eggs in one basket."
Tell that to the mother hen…
she knows to put all her eggs in one hole
and sit on it herself…
discipline, dedication, focus,
will hash her future

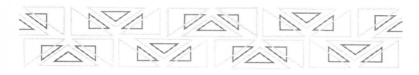

I believe to know suffering you will have to know her best friend true courage...just a stumble...get back to balance

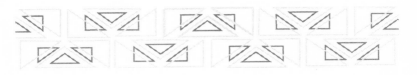

When I view love...I see so many little things that make love grow big

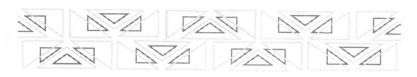

Knowledge will give you power, but character will give you respect

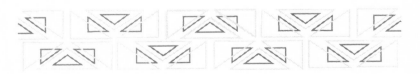

In order to get some coconut from the tree you
must wrap your legs,
locking your ankles together and your arms,
to climb to your destiny

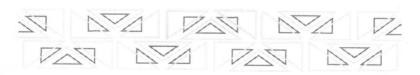

If someone bleeds for you...give them some tissue

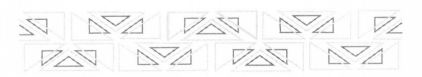

*How can you sleep under the mango tree and
not expect to get hit by a mango*

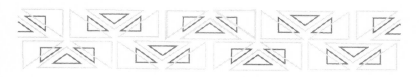

The only passport I will need now...is a smile

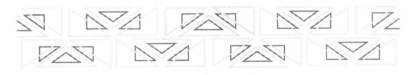

I'm in love with the word dandyism...
it makes mystery look classy

You are the architect of your own health and disease and your desire to live is totally up to your truth within you

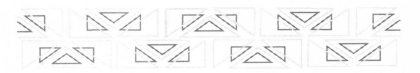

Pay attention please the earth is round...
when we are critical of each other,
when we are dishonest...
then our spiritual mind has attached to such
disease eventually resulting in
a bitter place...
please choose the truth

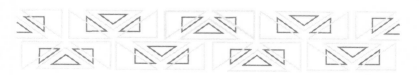

*Bulldoze your mind
when the road sign says dead end...*

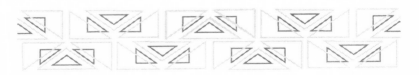

*Some how all that is around us everything is
connected somehow.
When we love each other, support each other,
existence will never die...so we are*

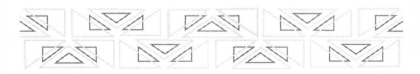

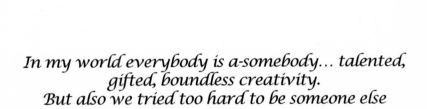

*In my world everybody is a-somebody... talented,
gifted, boundless creativity.
But also we tried too hard to be someone else*

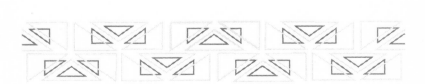

The bible doesn't say Adam and Eve lived happily ever after but it does say they were naked and unembarrassed...intimacy means we are safe enough to reveal our true wounds. In all its creative chaos...if we are totally free together those wounds will heal in due time...why do we give up too early?

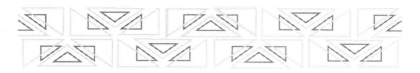

I have the greatest virus of mankind, love, and intend to infect all my encounters at any given time...

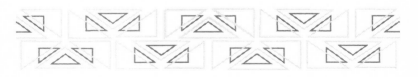

A painter's itch, your fingers are the ink, your heart, mind and soul are alert. Do you know what freedom is? Riding this vessel of good and evil we are all victim of experience. We've got fresh ice cubes for your glass the long day is over, shoot to the moon

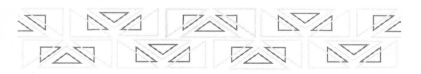

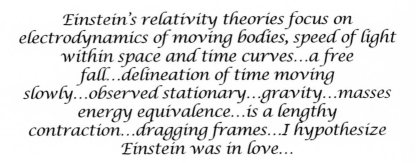

Einstein's relativity theories focus on electrodynamics of moving bodies, speed of light within space and time curves...a free fall...delineation of time moving slowly...observed stationary...gravity...masses energy equivalence...is a lengthy contraction...dragging frames...I hypothesize Einstein was in love...

Respect is the ultimate currency

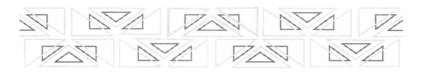

*The further you run from you the more
exhausted you are when you catch up to you*

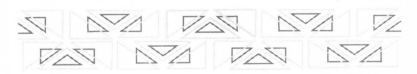

Violence is just fingertips away from a violin,
choose a better sound

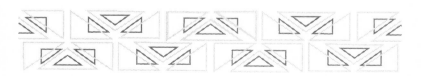

I first saw you, it wasn't my eyes that greeted you, it was my heart, not my hug, but my soul's arms, not your kiss, it was the imperfection of your tongue, licking up happiness, I wish cupid would shoot us everyday. Scarring us Valentine's love. Being human of God particles of infinite possibilities

When the truth is repressed it turns into darkness, negativity grows inside, smoldering, festering, then it leads to dysfunctional and destructive expression...hiding your darkness will also allow you to hide your light

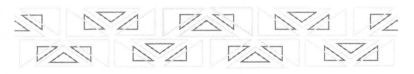

I'm all dressed up in an ascot matching socks, showing up for love, seeking authentic engagement before superficial agreement committed to truth, the keys to intimacy. Let's get naked and unembarrassed seeing each other's wounds and heal it...I want to see all your faces...my twin calls me Valentine...you can do the same

Let's stop sweeping our life challenges under the rug...it grows...our universe is holographic...in failing to complete in one area reflecting in all we do...one love

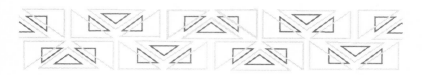

When there is not enough honesty or truth communicated between a couple, than negative masses are built up and bound to explode...sharing negativity means you are bad, it is toxin to the body...revealing brings healing...listening is light...non-judgment, truth moves on to a higher level, trust comes in

The ultimate truth is always light

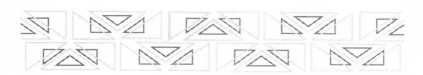

*The intellect must bow to the spiritual impulse
we are impregnated with divine ideas. In time
we will be ripe preparing to give birth to who
we were meant to be*

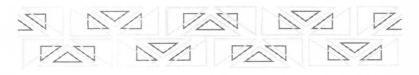

Those three little birds on Bob Marley's front step, one bird was his past burden, second was fear judging self, the third was a singing song of honesty for healing. The light is never far.

*I am a natural, doing surgery with the
world...giving words, hugs and kissing the dirt,
away liberating the soul
action does not speak louder than words,
a human voice infused with love, forgiveness,
acceptance, gratitude and happiness is deeper
than action*

All dreams begin with the dreamer, within the dream the essence of GOD gives you flight as morning rises we have to give it life.
My goal is to help free millions of minds from the world's expectation, maybe a billion. If they only knew they were trapped in systematic thoughts created by man

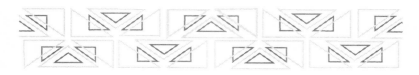

When we are all thinking alike,
doing the same thing,
talking the same thing,
than we are doing nothing

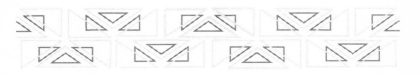

Love is the only language we all understand...
we must return to her...

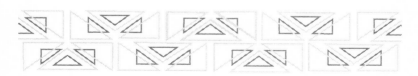

*Life is either a daring adventure or
nothing...security does not exist in nature...nor
do the children of man as a whole experience it,
avoiding danger is not safer in the long run
than exposure*

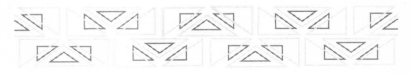

Some people have a PhD in worry, fear, anxiety, worry robs you...mother of cancer, sister of heart disease

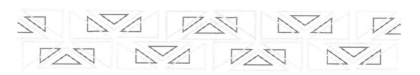

I'm not moved by what I see
I'm not moved by what I feel
I'm not moved by what I hear
But I am moved by what God's Word says

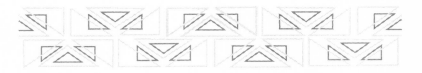

We must plant happiness in our souls, watering
it before enjoying the harvest of her. Man
cannot create happiness, just an agent of her

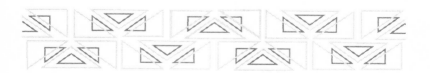

*While I'm searching for my big break,
my soul searches for me to break free.
Picture GOD breaking covenant...
cannot be...we are masterpieces*

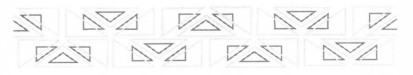

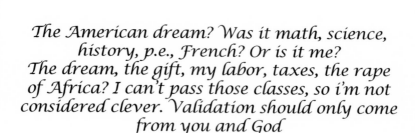

The American dream? Was it math, science,
history, p.e., French? Or is it me?
The dream, the gift, my labor, taxes, the rape
of Africa? I can't pass those classes, so i'm not
considered clever. Validation should only come
from you and God

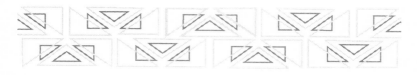

Into a vibration of fear, energy of caution, misleading tongue, schooling mankind, manipulation. Did you know in Mama's womb I regulated how much water went into my lungs for 9 months without Mama's help? Angelic we are

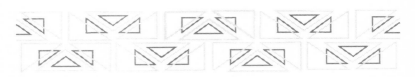

Everyday I lust for life, giving thanks, riding
with the sun, killing time, dead clock.
Enthusiast era, now or never, my will,
has become my clock

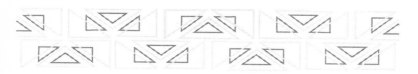

If you can speak something you never heard, write something you never read, you have done something rare

You were born an original,
don't die a cheap copy

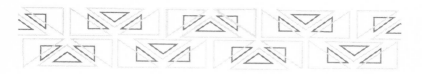

It's not what you are looking at that matters,
It's what you see

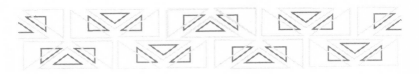

Many men go fishing all of their life without knowing that it's not fish they are after

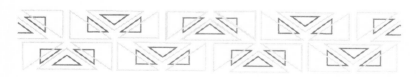

Not until we are lost can we begin to understand ourselves

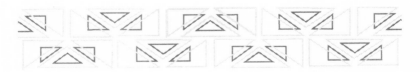

I may not touch love
but I smell her fragrance on you

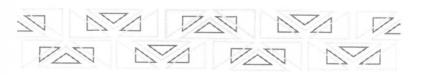

Grandma says, never look a horse straight in the mouth, never bend your head, just look the world straight in her face

*I wonder when man was made where GOD
began the measurement, heart, head, or legs...*

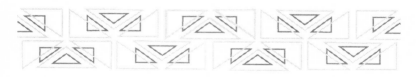

Obedience to man...will enslave your being with imaginary chains stifling your creativity...imagine putting your destiny of health and wealth in the hands of a being...start using your legs...and a faith of all senses...lose your eyes...use your heart

Make peace with who you are, hug yourself,
forgive yourself, contentment will enhance you,
those who make no mistakes are stagnant, keep
playing don't listen to the referee. You got the
right to be right and wrong

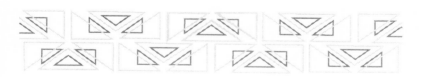

Today's remedy is compliment your lip's powers, touch, smile, get the beauty out of friends, loved ones, family, GOD was such a showoff when all creatures were created...

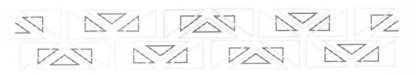

Falling in love has been getting a bad rap lately intellectual belief is an illusion, a state of mind, where you don't see the real human. Love is teaching me her lessons, a paradise retreat, dimensional bliss...no judges, just elder's praises...falling asleep to reality...no guilt or ego...the moon the only target

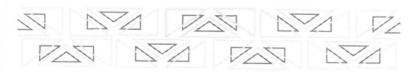

You are perfect as the inner core of all mankind...shoot for the moon...if they need to find you...they will need a heart shuttle to reach you

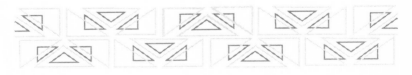

Law of success,
what you plant is what you eat

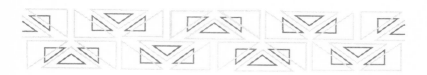

Recession is outbreak of fear...a sickness that crawls into your soul when encountered...people are infected...deeply with their soul by it...fear movement similar to a serpent...squeezing your peace, life, hope, view to live, meditate on your strength...get it out...contact your source set your frequency to GOD's tune

Wash limited thoughts with beauty soap...
she'll find you

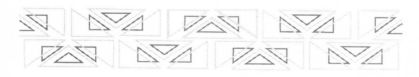

Freedom is misunderstood today, freedom is not a feeling, freedom is not sex, drugs, vodka. Freedom is the right decision, right choices, discipline, dedication to hard work, values, integrity in which we stand...for a life that can't be bought...witnesses...Mr. Marley, Malcolm, Martin, Michael, M. Ali, Marvin

*Your tongue can be like a needle, she stings
without a trace of blood*

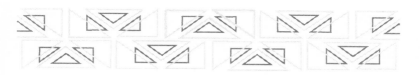

This is one of the most silent killers of the mind…doubt…attacks your heart, destroys relationships, friendships, kills without drawing blood. Believe in people before they are successful

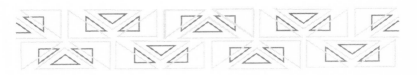

When your frequency is set on gratitude for
where you are in the universe than by law of
karma and attraction you get abundance

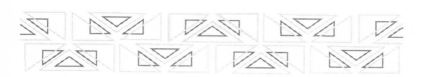

If man can conquer his desired mind to enlightenment...than all life virtues will naturally chase him...

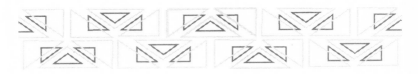

Those who are free resent...
bad thoughts, bad energy, gossip, avoid places
that steal their peace in practice,
but love to open their heart window, wine and
dine to the moonlight, love the voices of the
spirit, guiding to the truth

You cannot love a person, show affection, desire them, montage their beauties…unless you have that poetry within yourself…indeed you must

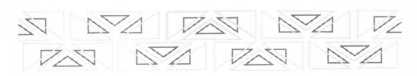

Depend on a human government for education,
knowledge, work and freedom
There goes your recession
Find your salvation in your abilities…
"you" in business

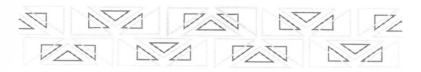

A kind gesture...a loyal heart, speaking honor to one another, helping each other, compassion, tolerance, unity, these are the fuels to get

Nyemah

*I Stevie Wonder if Richard Wright's good deeds
and patience ever got him a lot of money or
maybe his only good was good results*

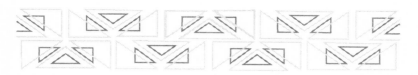

Why did they tell us to grow up? We didn't want
to grow up. For growth itself contains
a germ's awareness

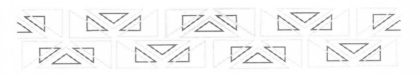

We must believe that every problem brings an
amazing gift...just unwrap it...learning is
finding out what you already know

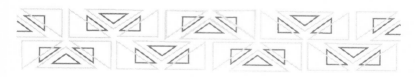

Your soul mate is the one who brings seeds of life to your life

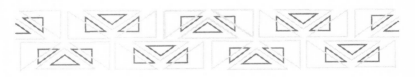

This is the moment, when ink becomes hugs,
pages become kisses,
when the lines are flowers of a Persian garden,
Words are like a dream you just touch when my
writings become places of blue sky, laughter,
love, freedom, no obligation to mankind, we
thank GOD for sharing this journey with us

My only purpose is for you to make a decision, show you the truth of choice, no preaching, just asking you to look in my window, architected by pain, touched by GOD's definition, finding essential points to life, happiness, self empowering, growth, gratitude, no need for a PhD, or Masters, I dare you to try it

Many people have the wrong idea of what constitutes happiness...it is not through self-gratification but through a worthy purpose

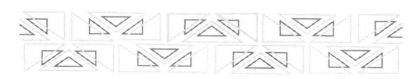

The only valuable reality is intuition

*My only celebrity, is me, my grandma, my
friends and the people I'm suppose to meet*

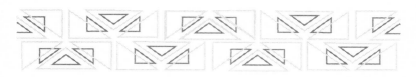

How did we get in this mess? Laboring, working hard just for a break, luck to come knocking? "Energy" changes your channel and frequencies. A station filled with feeling, dreaming bigger, own every moment

*Your dreams should be bigger than
your memories*

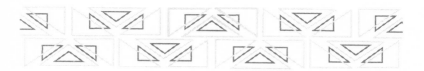

Dark seekers seek happiness in the distance. The light seekers grow happiness under their feet

Love pushes us in the arms of philosophy...to hold dignity, to know truth of our existence...ending the chaos in our daily life...the noisy world...philosophy's main focus is thought risen higher...beyond the places of scientist and man made, so let's think good thoughts of each other...thoughts that make us feel wealthy...like a treasure island is in your backyard

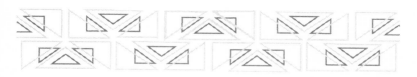

*Fear is a weapon of that voice in your head,
triggers sounds like, if…maybe…should…could…I
can't…never…blinding you of seeing that you
are part of the earth's atom*

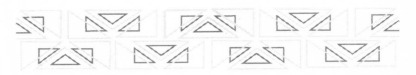

Our footprint in the sand molds us as our
thoughts follow the shadows of our life,
as you speak you act...lights, camera, action,
follow your destiny...we think it, we become it

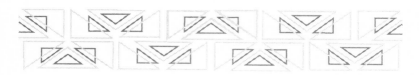

Jesus was a carpenter, owned a pair of sandals,
prayed for the men that tortured him...stone to
the thrown...Gandi sewed his own
clothes...fasted for humanity.
Today would they be considered successful?
At times wealthy men don't have a dollar
while all the poor man has is greed

We should never speak defeated words. Your
tongue is your prophet...your words are your
seeds, planted in the invincible soil
energy...watering the intangible...removing the
weeds that stifle growth...your tongue needs you

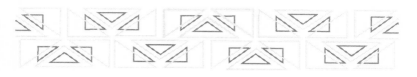

*The last thing that will fall out of my pocket
will be hope*

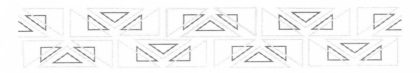

*How is it you want my best but you pay me less,
when my best is my health, not my wealth,
you must not know my worth, maybe you don't
know values, or am I a solid rock to build on*

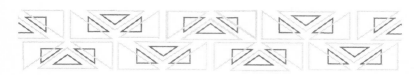

We learn the more friends we have the higher
we are...it's not about the quantity of your
circle but in truth the quality...

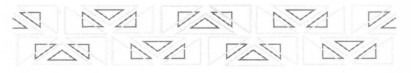

We believe in you, we trust your creativity,
there are no ages, we allow mistakes, with
society there are no second chances, we give
chances, the only things that are worth doing
are impossible, I'm possible, try it for the 1,777
time, keep on trying, says the whisper people in
our heads

*Growing up everything I did was bad, today
that bad enhances my character, that bad helps
me confront adversity, that bad helps me to
know my strengths and weaknesses… I am bad and
I love being bad*

The ocean is always blue, it never bothered her
about how many lives she took, or how much
dirt gets inside of her and her choices are always
blue…and we can vacation to see
her proof

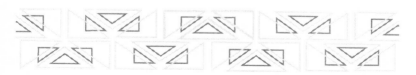

Excuse me Mr. Intentional, I don't want your freedom, if your freedom only permits me to be perfect with no mistakes...uh oh...he's losing control again

Blow your nose? What about your mind!
Dream!

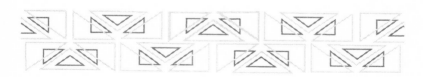

Thanks to my teachers,
but I would have enjoyed
Faith 101
Hope 202
Life 303
Believe in Me 404
Rather than listen to Sigmund Freud's
discoveries

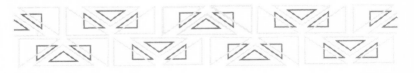

To most people the saying to use someone carriers a negative connotation but I don't see it that way. To abuse someone is negative, but to use is necessary and if you can't be used you are use less

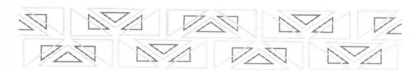

When fear knocks send faith to open

Tossing up a coin is like life, you can spend it the way you wish but you can only spend it once

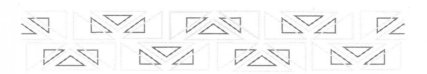

I see the light, the good, the bad, in all things
mostly overstanding the meaning of true love.
Surpassing those conditions

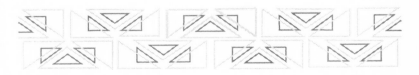

Every moment in your life is connected to the motion of your heart, thought, words, you may laugh if I tell you, you can create your world as God created the world with words in His image

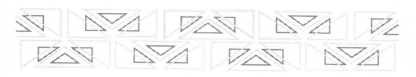

There is no growth without change, no change without fear or loss, and no loss without pain

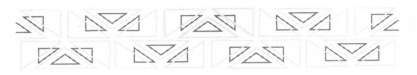

Pain birth the willingness to listen

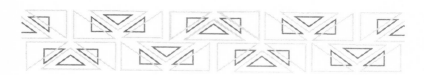

GOD is interested in changing me more than my
circumstances. He's firing where I am weakest
so I can discover my true strength in GOD

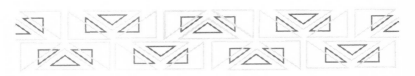

A man doesn't submit to his wife's lead but submits to her needs

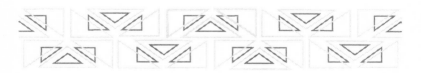

The most beautiful gift I learned from Kunta Kinte is name. So protect it because it is the last gift you will receive after death calls

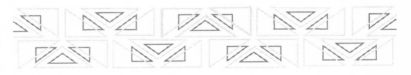

*Let them laugh at you, you stand for something,
they stand for nothing, that's why they fall
for anything*

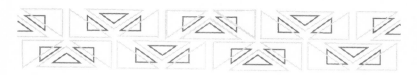

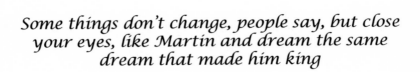

Some things don't change, people say, but close your eyes, like Martin and dream the same dream that made him king

Every time the clock turns there is an opportunity, tick, tock, tick, tock, each second, minute, unfolds a gift from GOD, it's called moment

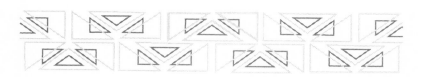

*Fools are those who have conclusion
before information*

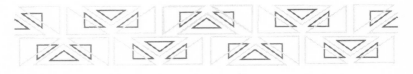

What ever you look at the most, listen to the most, will get in your spirit and then overcome your heart

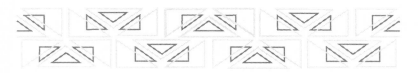

It's not the addition that enhances your life, it is the subtraction that enhances your life

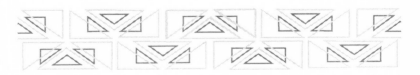

GOD does not reach the ones that are full of self,
rather, the one who humbles himself

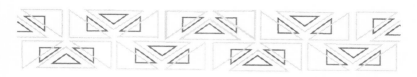

Some people feel that Sunday is the only day to be holy, to me being holy is Monday through Saturday, this is where GOD's grace is

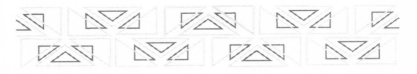

Every morning, I ask GOD: Whose life can I give hope to? This is where the wealth and the merit lies, this is how we affect life

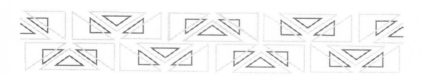

You cannot live a perfect day without doing something for someone who could not repay you

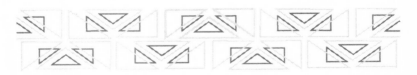

The best things in life are not free, that's a fact,
facts can be changed, that's not the truth, truth
cannot be changed

Follow GOD and the things your heart desires
will follow you

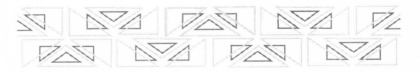

Don't tell GOD what you want, ask GOD what He expects from you

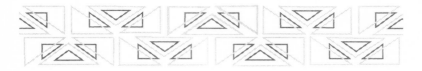

*Some people believe maturity starts with age,
but to me being responsible for your actions and
response is true maturity*

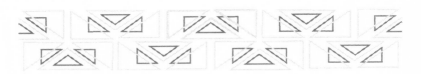

The happiest people don't necessarily have the best of everything, they make the best of the littlest things they have

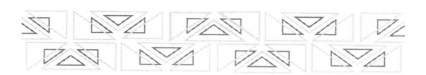

*Conquer you, the pot of gold is within you, it
needs to be on lock, leave the world to be*

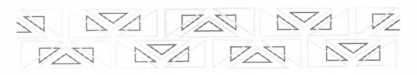

Trouble will show you true friends

Storms strip trees that have dead branches so
they grow new branches of strength

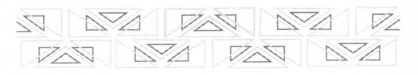

Buoyancy: the tendency or capacity to remain
afloat in a liquid, or rise in air or gas. So be
buoyant in life: lightness of spirit - cheerfulness

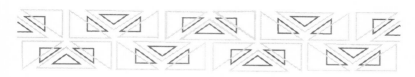

This world taught us about reward and merit, increases our growth by seeking true self, being able to walk your journey and knowing how to fail will lead you to your glory

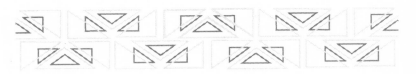

How you endure your storm determines your journey of destiny

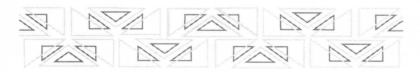

Great souls are grown through struggles, and storm, and season's suffering. Be patient with this process. Hope brings purity

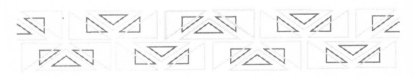

I am an artist, activist, abolishing the thoughts
that decrease our birth rates
I am you

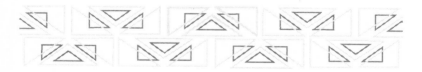

The Bible = Joy, Hope, Prosperity, Life, Faith, Health, this book talks back. Quiet your soul. True silence is where GOD is

Reality...what is reality? Is it something you feel for a moment? Then tomorrow that feeling is gone? So reality is simply feelings you emphasize. Emphasize on making it feel real. Then if that feeling is replaced with something good then that reality is gone. Reality is not true it can be changed

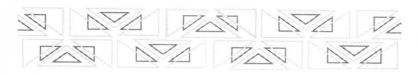

Think, and you will not move, you should move and think

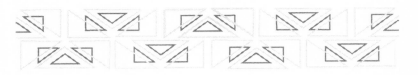

Excuses are the enemy of change

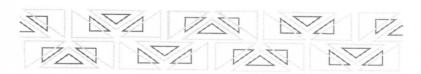

What you do not master will master you

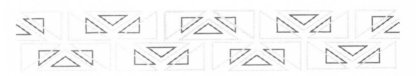

Faith creates miracles

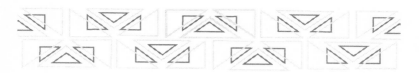

People work hard to obtain wealth,
forgetting their health,
to then spend the wealth to get health

*I feel the things that are not seen are greater
than the things that are seen*

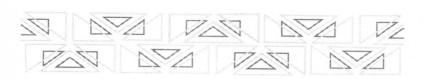

Trust is the highway to continuous triumph

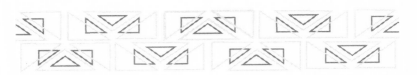

GOD's blessings are not from money and material things, but from the power to conquer

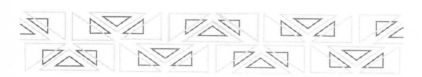

Trusting GOD enhances peace, self-control and confidence. Everything will be fine.

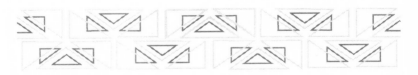

Doesn't matter how much you pay for those shoes, it will still touch the dirt. Only when you have nothing can you really appreciate and know true art from the heart

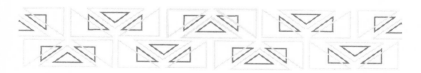

*We do what we have to do
to do what we want to do*

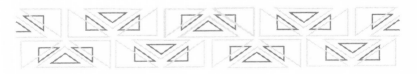

You will not posses if you do not pursue

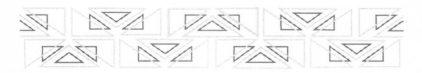

Don't be afraid of the deep,
faith without work is dead

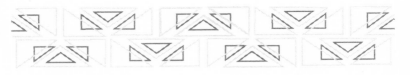

If you love life don't waste time. For time is what life is made up of.

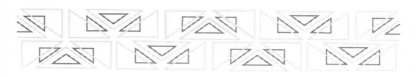

Every set back is the set up for a come back

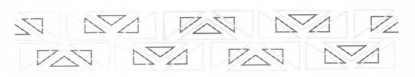

If you don't conquer your fears you will pass it on to your children as their parents passed it on to them. Conquer your fears

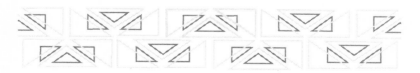

Showing off is a fool's idea of glory

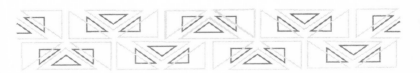

To hell with circumstances, I create
opportunity. Notice that the stiffest tree is most
likely to crack while bamboo bends with
the wind

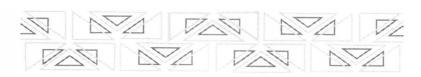

*Let your mind be formless, shapeless, like water.
Water in a cup becomes a cup. Put water in a
teapot it becomes a teapot. In a bottle, water
becomes the bottle. Be like water*

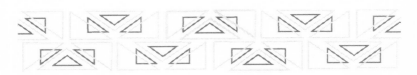

I don't know if success has a key, but I definitely know the key to failure is listening to other people

Take no thoughts of who is right or wrong or who is better than...be not for or against

Always be yourself, express yourself, have faith in you, do not go out and try to duplicate a successful personality

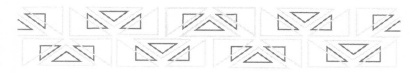

The less effort the faster and more powerful you will be

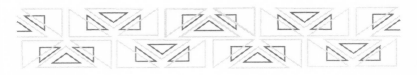

Only when you have put your knees
before God, then you can under-stand man

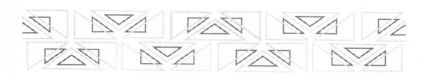

About the Author

Nyemah was raised in Liberia during the Liberian Civil War. He spent two difficult years alone as a child in a refugee camp in Sierra Leone. Although surrounded by negativity and death Nyemah spoke words of life to help keep himself alive every day. Through God and the help of Amnesty International Nyemah arrived in the United States-malnourished and sick with jaundice and malaria-given two weeks to live. His inner strength and determination prevailed as he overcame the many obstacles in his life. While artistry and writing are his passion, his mission in life is to share a message of happiness and inner strength.

To order additional copies of

Illuminate Within

have your credit card ready and call
From USA: (800) 917-BOOK (2665)
From Canada: (877) 855-6732

or e-mail
orders@selahbooks.com

or order online at
www.selahbooks.com

Books are also available through your
local bookstore in the US and Europe

CPSIA information can be obtained at www.ICGtesting.com
Printed in the USA
BVOW010529211211

278847BV00001B/1/P